Olga Sorokina

# *The* SKETCH

## Interior Design Drawing

2016

Olga Sorokina, «*The* SKETCH»

## Copyright © 2016 by Olga Sorokina. All rights reserved.

www.olgaart888.com
olgaart888@gmail.com

# Contents

# About this book

Meet this very actionable and fun book which, if you work with, will entirely change the way you present your interior design projects and, possibly, your entire creative life. I wrote this book specially for interior designers as well as interior design students who are new to freehand sketching and want to master this amazing skill in order to enhance their presentation skills.

Here you will find a lot of tools, tips, and tricks on freehand sketching. There are many useful and effective exercises plus my personal secret tips on how to make the most out of your presentation. We will also look into different sketching techniques used by famous hand renderers and hopefully you will learn a lesson or two from them. Written with a good sense of humour, the book shows the reader fun and lesser known side of interior design profession. Richly illustrated, this book will be a great source of inspiration to you, and hopefully it will become a permanent reference on your desk.

Having read this book you will:

◆ Understand how to construct different types of perspectives and practice by creating your first sketch of a living room in 1-point perspective.
◆ Create a beautiful and expressive sketch plan.
◆ Master different handrendering techniques.
◆ Bonus: you will have significantly more fun, confidence and freedom while working on your next interior design project.

**Have a great time and enjoy the journey!**

Author, Olga Sorokina

# About the author

Olga Sorokina is an interior designer, a visual artist and an author of sketching training eCourses for designers. She graduated with honors from The St Petersburg Stieglitz State Academy of Art and Design (MA, Interior Architecture and Furnishings, 2004-2010). She is a winner of numerous international prizes for interior design and architecture. Since 2014, she develops sketching and hand rendering courses that have been a tremendous success and benefited hundreds of students.

Website: www.olgaart888.com

Instagram: olgaart888

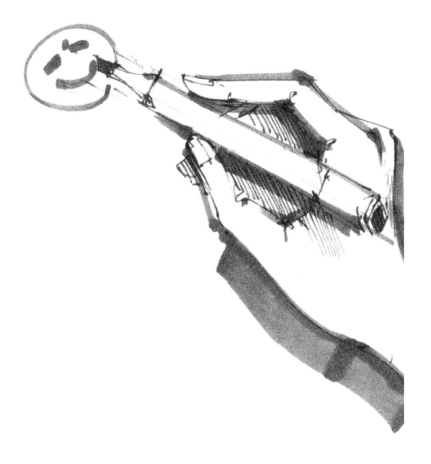

# Words of gratitude

I want to thank all the wonderful and talented people whose works and knowledge helped me in writing this book.

Special thanks to my husband and my dear parents who supported me throughout. I want to express my gratitude to my teachers from the best Art Academy in Russia (St Petersburg Stieglitz State Academy of Art and Design) for passing their priceless knowledge to me.

Very special thanks to my dear friend Nadejda Alexander, without your help this book would remain uncompleted.

And, of course, I want to thank all my students who inspired me to write this book.

**Thank you!**

# INTRO

---

Where the main message of
the book is put forward and
words of gratitude are said

# Word of introduction from the author

*To my students*

Hello, my dear readers. I am extremely glad to get in touch with you on the pages of this book, where I am going to tell you about freehand sketching, a unique skill which is so important to all designers. I will show you basic hand rendering techniques and demonstrate my favourite materials that I use in my everyday sketching. There are chapters that you will find particularly interesting, like "The Masters", where I am going to reveal some of the secrets of freehand sketching techniques used by some of the greatest sketching artists.

This knowledge will form a solid theoretical and practical basis, on which you will be able to build your own original style. This book will enable you to represent your interior ideas in a new, completely spontaneous, freehand way. This material will provide you with a step-by-step guide to the amazing world of sketching.

I wrote this book with great inspiration and I very much hope that you will also feel these positive vibes. Basically, this is the main objective of the book: to unleash your creativity, as well as to inspire you, to get across to you my love for the art of sketching and perspective and, on the whole, to introduce you to the exquisite esthetic of hand rendering and skills that you will use in your interior design practice. For some of you, this book will be a genuine salvation from the overwhelming burden of computer technologies.

"The Sketch" is essentially a printed version of my eCourse on freehand sketching with markers for interior designers and interior design students. I tried to reflect here my experience of being a teacher of freehand sketching and systematize my knowledge in this field. It is interesting that among my students there are not only interior designers and architects, but also florists, stylists, fashion designers and other creative professionals. I also discovered that even economists, lawyers, diplomats and other professionals who were eager to try themselves in interior design also found this eCourse extremely helpful and were able to achieve spectacular results.

During my workshops and real life courses, a lot of ideas were generated that were easy to put in action and it is time for me to share them with you in this book. My experience as an interior design student in St Petersburg Stieglitz State Academy of Art and Design (MA in Interior Design, 2004-2010) is also reflected here, as well as more than seven years of working as an interior designer for private clients and companies. I can honestly say that this book is the essence of my skills and knowledge in sketching and I am so happy to share them with you. This book is packed with step-by-step recipes of well-done sketches that are accompanied by richly illustrated material.

I hope that having read this book some of you will be able to find an interesting job, refresh their approach to the interior design projects or successfully graduate from a design school or be able to enter their Dream University. And everyone, I am convinced, will fall in love with interior sketching and will gradually start making progress in this field. I am sure there are people, and maybe YOU are one of them, who are daydreaming about mastering a new creative profession, and sketching will definitely help them boost their talent and advance the process of becoming the best version of themselves.

Last but not least, sketching will provide you with a much more efficient and faster way to convey your ideas.

So my main message to you is this:

**Even if you have never drawn before you are more than capable of producing stunning sketches! Have no doubt about that!**

In making your first baby steps in sketching, you will benefit enormously from precise guidance and proven methodology presented in this book by dividing your creative path into milestones, which will eventually, but undoubtedly, lead you to your goals.

So please give me your hand and I will guide you to the Wonderful World of Sketching! On this path you are going to meet great masters of hand rendering and freehand sketching and get acquainted with drawing techniques, which will help you become a real professional.

This book will encourage you to draw and will help you to overcome any fears of drawing that many of you no doubt have. So if, while reading it, you feel a strong desire to draw, please follow it and do not hesitate to grab your pen (right now!) and welcome to the Wonderful World of Sketching!

Olga Sorokina, «*The* SKETCH»

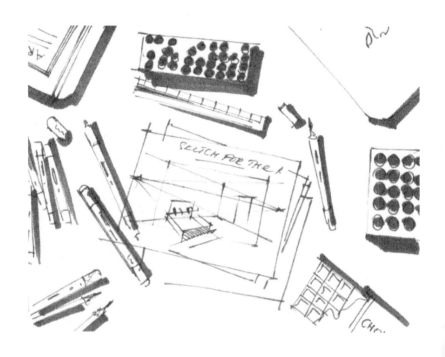

# SKETCHING

**01**

In which I explain what sketching is,
and how I came to do it and what is
the main aim of this book

# *1.1.* What is sketching?

Basically, it is about making a quick drawing, a study, which helps you to represent a design idea. And it has a plethora of applications:

**Travel sketching** (or sometimes city sketching): expressive, energetic and usually extremely fast drawings of architectural details, city views, restaurants, etc. It can be made both in open air ("pleinair" in French) and working from your memory – recollections of your trip when you are back at home, or using photos and creating compositions out of them. It includes "cafe sketching" as well.

**Fashion sketching**: people, fashion-looks and accessories. It is used mainly for illustrations or magazines, e.g. for brand promotion. It helps designers during the first stages of creation of their collections and helps introducing changes.

**Industrial Design sketching**: probably the most known and popular branch of sketching. Obviously, it was created by industrial designers; a good example is car sketching. In this case, all sketches are made with great speed and confidence.

The type of sketching we are going to study here is a little different, we will start by creating a precise measured perspective with help of scale rulers. This will be followed by freehand rendering which may take 2-3 hours, and for this stage we will be using markers. Once you have mastered the construction technique, you will develop the ability to produce quick freehand sketches of interiors, which is the ultimate goal of the entire book.

Sketching is an amazing skill which lets you transfer your design idea onto paper in the most fun, fast and effective way. In other words, sketching is a unique instrument for visualizing your concepts. Nowadays, it is associated mostly with such media as specialized professional markers, for example Copic, Stylefile, Chartpak, Promarkers, ZIG, etc. Actually sketching "palette" is very wide and versatile: you can start from scratch by using a pencil, charcoal or black liner and end up by using different types of colouring techniques, for instance watercolour, coloured ink and pastel or watercolour pencils. It is possible to mix different media, for instance markers + pastel or watercolour + coloured pencils. There are so many creative opportunities for you to test and explore! It is a good idea to try several and pick a couple of "favourites".

A range of this kind of media in the art-shops can impress and confuse at the same time. But don't worry, my friends, in the coming chapters I will recommend you a nice and compact set of marker colours, which I personally use most of the time. But why I do recommend markers? This is my answer: in my opinion, markers are the most easy-to-learn-how-to-use and easy to implement technique for beginners (especially in comparison to watercolour) and, at the same time, sketches done with markers usually look more vibrant. As a matter of fact, in my personal interior design practice, I used to use watercolour and coloured pencils for my drawings, whereas now I opted for markers only because I simply see how much better they perform on paper for interior design purposes.

The reason why sketching became so popular today among designers of all kinds not only in Russia, Europe, USA, Asia and the rest of the world is because artists nowadays tend to be overwhelmed by computer programs such as CAD, 3D Max and Maya. In the old days, artists were earning their bread by, literally, their hands and now they are desperately wishing to go back in time when ideas were transferred through hand drawing, which is far more natural and organic way of doing it.

Just take a look at what is happening right now in our creative lives: we rarely, if ever, write with a pen, and mostly type on a computer, iPad or iPhone. We do not send handwritten letters and cards anymore – epistolary genre is almost gone for good – and even our thoughts and ideas we capture in "Notes" on our iPhones. It seems that we have forgotten the meaning of "hand made", hand crafted, which is precious, because in creating it you include a piece of your heart, love and memories. Do you remember what we were told as children: "The best present is the one that is made by hands". There is a profound meaning in that. Just observe that we no longer "create" on paper but "work" on a computer, in Photoshop, Word or AutoCAD. The words we use, especially verbs, bear deep meaning. With that in mind, ask yourself, is it better to render or to hand-render; to work or to create? They say that 3D Max was invented by those who can not draw. Clearly, there is a number of advantages in using 3D and computer-generated imagery, but let us not lose the command of our hands and the link between the brain and the heart that hand drawing fosters.

# *1.2.* Types of sketching

As I mentioned before there are different types of sketching and here I would like to talk about each one in a little bit more debths. Let's take a quick look at the main features of most popular of them by splitting them into key concepts and key words.

### FASHION SKETCHING

For this type of sketching it is important to have a good understanding of human proportions (face and body). You should know how to stylize figures in your drawings. More often than not, body proportions are elongated in fashion sketching. For example, the total height of human body in fashion sketching is 10, 11 or even 12 times the height of a human head as opposed to real-life proportions of only 7.5 to 8 heights of a human head. The most important aspect of fashion sketching is to be able to capture a design idea in the best possible light. Hence a facial-portrayal of a human figure is usually not important. In this case it is critical to be able to deliver the idea of the designed collection to the best advantage. In fashion sketching it is important to bring the clothing design into focus, and a life-like portrayal of the figure is completely unimportant. You will also need to know how to convey through hand-render the look and feel of such materials and textures as skin, hair, different types of fabric, metal, etc.

### INDUSTRIAL SKETCHING

You will need the ability to draw objects in 3D, clearly showing their structural design and volume. In order to be able to render a professionally looking arrangement of component part on a page you will need firm grasp of the principles of composition. You will also need to perfect your technique and speed in order to develop assured line and confident hand. Most common materials that need rendering in industrial sketching are metal, plastic and glass.

## TRAVEL SKETCHING

In this type of sketching, the most important skill is to manage to convey the feel, the ambience of a place, to capture the flitting moment and, at the same time, to deliver correct scale and proportions of the object. More often than not, you will also need to be able to perform at high speed, as you will be sketching while travelling, while on the road, when you do not have several hours at your disposal the way it would have been the case with plain-air sketching. In this type of sketching it is important to grasp the intrinsic traits of the place you are observing and afterwards graphically stylize it in your drawing.

## INTERIOR SKETCHING

For this kind of sketching it is highly important to understand the laws of perspective and train your eye to judge scale and proportion. It is always good to be able to execute your drawings within different time frames, because sometimes you will need to draw your idea quickly in front of your customer. As an interior designer you should have an eye for beauty, a feeling for harmonious colours and a perfect palette. And, as in other types of sketching, you should be able to render a variety of materials such as fabric, wood, stone and glass.

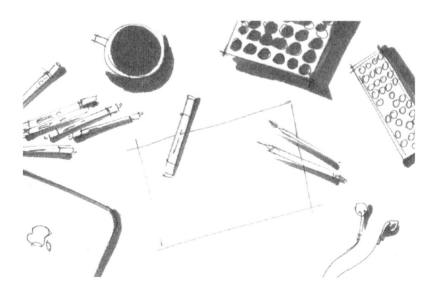

# *1.3.* How I came to sketching?

In fact, I have never parted ways with it. Drawings, plain-airs, designs, sketches, outlines, drafts – all these have been my close companions all my life. Throughout my education first at the Arts School for Children Alexandrino, followed by four years at the Arts and Aesthetics School on the Fontanka River and finally 6 years at the St Petersburg Stieglitz State Academy of Art and Design, I was always drawing, perfecting my technique, honing on my skills and hand confidence. I have been studying sketching all my life and even now I am continuing to refine my skills almost everyday.

I would admit that the system is somewhat inflexible in depth it lacks a modern approach and that is Russian Art Academies provide solid foundations, and exceptional old school education, particularly in academic drawing. In Russia, we are very proud of our cultural traditions and systematic in-depth, comprehensive approach to the artistic education.

Contemporary methods, marketing and brand-building are what I call "complimentary options", something that a designer can learn on his own using information on Internet, books or short courses. Technology is developing at a very fast pace, new teaching methodologies continue surfacing, but always remember that no skyscraper can be built without proper foundations so the core skills must be solid and comprehensive. What are the core skills? This are the necessary skills, the understanding of the essence of the subject, acquisition of the faculty of fast learning. For interior design, for instance, it is important to know history of arts, design principles, ergonomics, materials science, colour theory, understanding of materials, perfect command of perspective and shadow projections and drawing techniques. If it is fashion design, we need to know surface anatomy, materials, stylization techniques, sewing basics and pattern cutting etc.

Interior sketching is one of the key components of a successful and productive design practice. Masterful command of perspective, rendering and stylization are the tree main skills that you will need to develop in order to be successful at it. In fact, the sketching practice boils down to a certain sum of knowledge and skills, which are essential to professionalism and expertise. Do not be put off if you have never held a pencil in your life! Sketching is a skill which is entirely possible to learn and improve upon. Always rememberer if there is a will, there is a way.

During my years at the Stieglitz State Academy of Art and Design, majority of our time was spent on disciplines such as architectural drawing, perspective, academic drawing, designing, modeling, composition and colour serie. As you can see the programme was very intensive. That is why the course takes six years to complete, the sixth year being allocated to work on student's work diploma.

In this book I am going to give you the absolute essence of the knowledge required to become a successful practitioner of interior sketching. I adore the aesthetics of freehand rendering. In my opinion, it is a much more natural fluid and more vivid way of visual expression of an idea compared to a static dead looking 3D model that took a vast amount of your time and your nerves to produce. All painters and designers are in essence visual artists, as we constantly work with images. That is why it is so important for designers to have the ability to create a desired image on paper by hand in a fast and efficient way to demonstrate an idea simply and effectively. Nothing captures your client's imagination then when you start drawing right before their eyes.

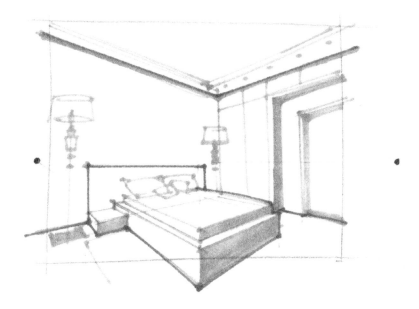

# My story

I was in my third year at the Art Academy when computer programmes invaded our academic life. As young creatives we were all completely fascinated by 3D Max, Photoshop, AutoCAD and it seemed impossible to ignore them when we were preparing our projects. We were given some basic instructions of these software packages at the Academy, and then some of us kept studying these programmes with the help of books and specialized courses. On the whole, a lot of time, effort and money were spent to master this software. Incidentally, many students were left dissatisfied when after having spent their money they felt they did not acquire profission command of the software. It is hardly surprising. This software suits a particular mind-set that is characteristic not so much of an artist, but of a technical professional, programmer. Have you noticed that most 3D Max professionals, visualizers and CAD operators are chiefly men? Perhaps, it is because men are more technically minded...

Over time, these programmes started to supersede hand rendering. During my last year at the Academy, I was working on my diploma, and in parallel I was free-lancing as a designer for a prominent firm. I regret to admit that I found myself drawing less and less, increasingly becoming a manager of my project rather than a designer. I felt let down, I was questioning if my chosen profession was no longer the right thing for me. Luckily I was well trained and I quickly rediscovered the link between my heart, my mind and my hand and since then I went on to uninstall all computer assisted design software. Incidentally, most of my students come to me with this exact problem. Interestingly, most of my students are women. The fact that you are holding this book in your hands indicates that you are at the same crossroads. I am delighted to say that there is a way out so let's get on and look at the profession of an interior designer.

# *1.4.* Who is an interior designer?

This is an important part and some of you may get upset when I dispel the myth that the interior design profession is about beauty and romantic appeal, but you better know the truth if you want to avoid a "blind date" disappointment. Interior design is not about pleasant meetings with customers in glamorous restaurants and elegant offices, reflecting on the subject of interior styles, choosing that ideal shade of taupe for the tiling in the bathroom, artistic inspiration and perpetual joy of creation. Well, some of it is, but it sums up to no more than 5% of the overall project scope. The rest of it is arduous daily routine: designer supervision at a construction site, naked concrete walls, breathing all this cement dust hanging in the air, speaking to often rude builders, managing orders, chasing suppliers generally putting out fires on a daily basis.

To give a complete image: an interior designer is an all-round craftsman, multi-armed, multi-legged and multi-brained. He bears in his mind plethora of diverse information: starting with yesterday's conversation with the customer, requests from his wife, children and his dog, visits to a tile store, sanitary equipment showroom, lighting shop, reviewing a quotation and negotiating with construction supervisors, and rows about missed deadlines. One other aspect that is rarely mentioned is the futile struggle to foster a good taste in customers trying to persuade them that rhinestone and crimson velvet from a luxurious Italian palazzo looks like unabashed kitsch in the context of a city apartment. At the same time, you will need to find time and energy to visit a great many interior design exhibitions, many of which take place at least twice a year, in order to be well-versed in new technologies and materials. As you can see, it is a very vibrant and eventful life. The most exhausting part of it all is relentless multitasking and we now know that it is the least efficient way of getting things done and by far the most draining. At the same time, creativity was supposed to fit in all this somehow and be the essence of the designer's occupation, given that he is an artist, "designer engineer", as it is inscribed in my diploma.

The fact of life is: a designer is often a project manager, a director, an author, a supervisor and a diplomat, all rolled into one. Of course, this definition also applies to any self-employed designer, or an owner of a small design studio, or a freelancer, or any other professional who work for himself, rather than a company.

In the midst of the hustle and bustle, when you have this, that or the other place to rush to, dozens of appointments to keep, panicking clients to calm down and a builder to explain of this things to, your energy dissipates very quickly and your stamina very soon wanes, days are slipping away imperceptibly, and almost nothing is done... Does that sound like the way things are sometimes in your case? Cheers! This means it is the right time for you to get away from it all, take it easy, recharge your batteries and discover a new way to spur your creativity and awaken your inspiration.

In fact, this is exactly where sketching will help you. Concentrate on your creativity, on drawing, and you will see the progress straight away along with rapid professional growths. Being a creative person, a designer must always feel that he or she is constantly developing and growing professionally.

I think it is of paramount importance to a designer or an architect – the ability to express ideas on paper using just a pencil. Having graduated from the Arts Academy, I was astonished to find out that some designers were completely incapable of drawing and many of them have never even tried to, commenting that the main thing was the ability to use appropriate computer programmes, knowledge of building principles, regulations and materials. It is beyond doubt that it is highly important to be an expert of your craft, a professional in your field. And in real life it is also vital to be good at maintaining relations with customers and construction workers, and to have a leadership talent.

You gain **respect in your** clients' eyes when he or she sees a complex interior being artfully created by you and there is nothing that proofs your professionalism and creativity further than if you drawing a sketch right in front of the client during a meeting. It does the trick 100% of the time!

Ask yourself: what is it precisely that I want to do? What is missing from my creative process? What would be my ideal creative process? If you are a computer geek – there's no problem. However, if you are perturbed by the feeling that something is missing, that you are disconnected from your work, that you no longer enjoy coming to the office and that everything became a routine, it means you need to discover a new way and acquire new knowledge and skills. You need to find a way to re-introduce elegance spontaneity and joy back into your profession.

# Getting back to my story

At one point, I noticed that I had given up on drawing. Really, one not so fine days I realized that I was almost perpetually seated in front of my computer, embroiled in a battle with 3D and AutoCAD, that all the time I was googling some sanitaryware, analyzing business proposals and quotations and had completely given up on creative side of things. It just hit me: "Did I spent 6 years at the best Russian Art Academy for nothing?! What was the point of it all? Was it even worth it? And what about my talent, my artistic flair?" I had a feeling I was betraying something fundamental within myself. And at that moment I clearly saw that this was a problem that I had to address immediately.

About the same time, I received a call from a friend of mine who asked me if I could give her a few interior drawing classes (Tanya, thank you!). That's when it dawned on me that lots of designers felt the same way: a desperate lack of freehand drawing skills which was a key creative component of their work which was missing and that I was not the only one tormented by the problem of being constantly seated in front of a computer.

That was how my interior sketching course came to life. Soon after I started to give classes to individual designers from different cities and countries, offering them training on sketching and rendering. After that I began to give classes to groups of students, and my online courses were accompanied by live workshops in Moscow and my home town St Petersburg. At present moment, as I am writing this book, I want to systematize a plethora of information on interior sketching that I am going to distill down to the essential knowledge, to the gist of it all, and represent the material in a clear, understandable and exciting way.

# *1.5.* Summary of the Chapter

The main message of this book is this: " You Can Do Professional Sketching"! This is a new skill which can be learned and mastered with frequent practice. It is no different from learning a new language or a dance.

**You can excel at sketching even if you have never held a pencil in your hands!**

This is because interior sketching is 50% mathematics and 50% learnable techniques. In the next chapter we will look at various techniques used by some of the best sketching artists, discover what they are and why they are so effective.

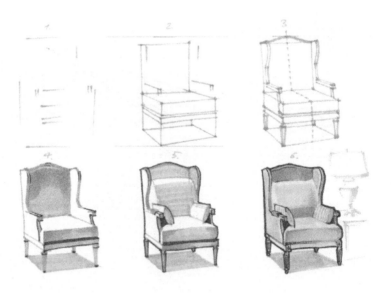

# MASTERS

## 02

In this chapter I will tell you about four world gurus of sketching and will acquaint you with their techniques. You will also learn why Art Academies insist that their students do copies of the masters and of what use this may be to us

# 2.). Gurus of sketching

When you are starting to learn something, it is of key importance that you learn from the best in the field – this way you will set yourself a good benchmark from the outset to strive towards. In this book I would like to tell you about four world class masters. Each one of them has his own style and expression and unique techniques, which can be identified, analysed and deployed in your own practice.

**Always ask yourself: What is it that I like so much about this sketch/drawing/ artist/project?**

Be observant and attentive, be the constant questioner, look beyond the first impressions, pay attention to details, always try to get to the heart of the matter. Ask yourself: " What is so special about this work?" Is it the well-chosen palette, or delightful light effects, or, maybe, unconventional drawing techniques? Constantly study, train your brain to analyze, and your eyes to observe. Having figured out the technique, use it in your drawing, play with it, find out how much it is to your liking, whether it is your thing or not. In this case, the goal is not to copy the style of an artist, and not to imitate the technique thoughtlessly and indiscriminately in your drawing, but to experiment with a technique, try your hand at it, reveal your personality through it, and this is how a new technique will eventually emerge which will be inimitable and entirely your own. We are all different and drawing reflects our personalities. Freehand drawing vividly reveals and brings out the unique character of a person. No other human being thinks, feels, analyzes and draws in absolutely the same way.

Talking about copying: why do you think all Art Academies teach their students to copy works of old masters (e.g. Rubens, Leonardo and Michelangelo)? Moreover, copying is an essential part of their curriculum. This is because: the most amazing thing happens, when a student copes a work of a great master – he comes into contact with the way of thinking of the genius. In imitating the strokes of the master, your hand sends signals to your brain and you start to understand the thought process that went into creating a particular painting. You follow the movements of his pencil, and, therefore, of his thought. Automatically, your hand starts to memorize effective techniques and methods. You start getting a better grasp of proportions, well-chosen angle view, and well arranged compositions. By doing so you are developing the so called "body memory". Your hand gives the brain a whole new picture of the world, and that's how your own technique evolves, it starts developing times and times faster, it becomes very confident, because it acquires a powerful capacity of old masters.

We are going to try the same thing. Let's examine a few works by sketch masters from various countries, who are undoubtedly the gurus of sketching and who have spent years developing their skills. Let us examine works of these masters coming from different countries.

Note: Illustrations in this chapter are my copies of masters' works.

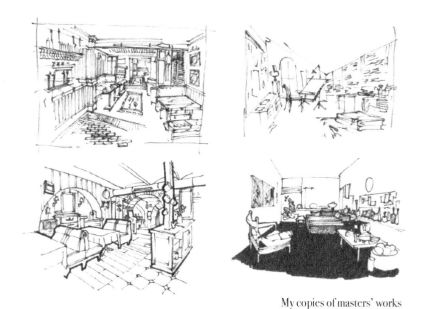

My copies of masters' works

# 2.2. Richard Chadwick

Here comes the first master that I want to introduce you to, Richard Chadwick. He comes from Manchester. I would like to quote here his words about the art of sketching:

*As an antidote to the ubiquitous – and to my mind anodyne – computer produced visuals, these are all drawn by hand, mainly pen and marker renderings, capturing the energy of the moment and generally looking far more dynamic than anything produced by a computer programme. A return to hand crafted values offers a way forward from an entirely technologically based society and the tactile feel of pencil on paper has its own reward.*

Chadwick has been in the profession for many years. He worked both as an architect and as an interior designer. Now he mostly focuses on freehand visuals. In his interviews he says that he usually uses A3 sheets of paper for drawings and spends 2 to 3 hours on a drawing on average. You can see that this is extremely quick as compared to a rather lengthy process of 3D visualization. His sketches are so very full of life and energy! His portrayal of the feel, the ambience of a place is absolutely splendid.

**What is special about Chadwick's technique?** Markers, partial colour filling, focusing on the central part of the composition, freehand lines, no rulers. No less important is the speed. His lines are very free, never perfectly straight and sometimes, even they are slightly bent, give the overall composition the "fish eye lens effect".

Chadwick's knowledge of perspective principles is so profound that he does not hesitated to break them in order to achieve his vision. Sometimes you will find several horizon lines in his drawings and the diagonals often do not meet at the vanishing point, despite all that, his drawings always feel correctly constructed and full of emotionality, liveliness and dynamism.

**What can you try to do the way Chadwick does?** As a rule, it is the focal point of a drawing (its background) that he fills with colour, whereas the foreground could be executed in thin lines. Try to identify one sort of your overall composition and focus on colouring only the central part. By applying colour only to certain parts of a drawing you will save both time and markers. An interesting trait of his drawing is that when Richard Chadwick makes textures and works over detail, he shows only fragments of them (for example, only fragments of tiling on the floor). This is the most effective application of the 'understatement' technique, and lots of areas in his drawings are only marked with thin lines. The master uses a very limited colour palette in one sketch which is usually 5 to 7 markers.

**Favourite subjects**: bars, restaurants, cafes.

**Homework**: do a copy of 1-2 of Chadwick's interior sketches. This will help you to acquire a quick and impressive drawing technique. Carefully observe and analyse everything that he does as go along.

My copy of master's work

## 2.3. Sergio Rodrigues

Our second master is a furniture designer and an architect Sergio Rodrigues. He is a legend in Brazil and his work is recognised world over.

**Technique, practical training**: favourite materials of the master are liners, black Chinese ink, sometimes watercolour. His drawings are very expressive and their energetic graphics falls into the category of interior illustrations. His technique very much resembles 'the wire work' method where all objects are carefully inked over contour and detailed.

**Contributions to your collection of techniques**: notice how Rodrigue's drawings have distinct foreground and background. The lines of the objects in the foreground are thick and rich in colour, whereas in the background lines are lighter. Notice how he applies flat colour for example to the floor and by doing so, he accentuates the contrast and graphic feel of his sketches.

**Favourite subjects:** restaurants, bars, residential, furniture.

**Homework:** analyze the master's technique, do a copy of one of his works.

My copies of master's works

## **2.4.** Albert Hadley

One of the best-known American decorators of all times, Hadley worked for such celebrity clients as Jacqueline Kennedy, Oscar de la Renta, as well as vice-presidents and ambassadors. Hadley played an exceptional role and made a significant contribution to the XX-th century American interior design.

**Technique, practical training:** sketches made by the master are for the most part very graphic in style and are executed in pencil, Chinese ink and stylus. Albert Hadley usually used toned drawing paper and was famous for his incredible speed of drawing. He had his sketches finished in a matter of seconds. This proves his great mastery – speed and accuracy of performance. Have a look at his drawings. How vigorous, energetic, fluent and lucid they are, and, at the same time, how exceptionally well he renders an idea and feel of a prospective interior, the ambiance of a space.

**Contributions to your collection of techniques**: Albert Hadley never used rulers or rubbers when drawing. This can teach us a good lesson – try and learn to render your idea on paper in the most quick, clear-cut, articulate and expressive way, almost with one stroke of pen.

**Favourite subjects of sketches**: interiors of Victorian houses, libraries.

**Homework**: do a copy of one of the drawings by the master using liner or pen.

My copy of master's work

# 2.5. Michelle Morelan

And to finish our list of gurus for this book, let me introduce to you a Canadian woman-designer Michelle Morelan. She grew up on the West Coast of Vancouver Island and early on she understood how the aesthetics of nature and architecture intertwine in harmony to a deeply satisfying effect. This is the reason why peace and tranquility of natural way of living have found their way into all of her drawings with accentuated textures, natural materials, open spaces and enjoyable colour palette, mostly consisting of sandy, earthy and woody colour tones.

**Technique, practical training**: the master uses a combination of techniques to create hybrid sketches. As a rule, she constructs a space in a 3D programme (such as "Sketch Up"), and then she hand-sketches and colours interesting angles of perspective with markers.

**Contributions to your collection of techniques**: like Chadwick, Michelle Morelan has a very restrained colour palette. I would call her technique "minimalistic sketching": often only one or two materials are accentuated (frequently these are wood and stone).

**Favourite subjects of sketches**: spacious interiors of countryside houses.

**Homework**: do a copy of one of Morelan's sketches.

My copy of M. Morelan's work can be found in Chapter 7.

# MATERIALS

## 03

This chapter will tell you what materials you will need to start sketching, which brands of markers would be the best choice, what I personally use in my sketching routine, what are my favourites and how lucky we are to have them!

# 3.). Marvel of markers

You have no idea how lucky we are to have markers! During my years at the Art Academy (2004-2010), there were no markers available for purchase in Russia. Nobody knew of their existence and classic hand rendering techniques were the norm: watercolour, Indian ink, rapidograph pens, tracing paper, coloured pencils. We used blow dryers to dry wet paint coats to speed up the process, and razor blades to repair mistakes. All kinds of things were deployed, many of which the younger generation of designers would not have even heard of. From that point of view, markers are faster and easier to draw with and we are fortunate that there there's a diverse array of splendid materials available in art shops intended to help us. This is an ideal sketching tool made specifically for designers!

## An architectural graphics case from my student experience

In the olden days if you wanted to do architectural graphics or a coloured drawing you had to: fix a watercolour paper leaf onto a sketch board, securing it on the board to stay in position lest it should crinkle when moistened by water. You would then plot the perspective of a space. Then, coat after coat, you would cover the drawing with watercolour, wait till the paint was completely dry, then apply shadows. After that, you would apply glazing (a technique of applying paint, coat after coat, to intensify the three-dimensional effect), and, finally, you would do textures of materials and details. As you can see, it all sums up to a rather laborious and time-consuming process.

The cost of a mistake was very high: if you happened to accidentally let a drop of Indian ink fall on the leaf, you would have to start all over again. Of course, you could sometimes go over with a razor blade to clean up, but this would more often than not damage the texture of the paper. And if you had gone too far having mixed too many colours, you could have ended up with a 'muddy' effect: colour that is flat lucking air, transparency and complexity. In such cases it was possible to wipe 'muddiness' off with a sponge, but the impression of lightness and freshness would go, and work would have 'tormented' and 'tired' look.

Let me tell you a story from my personal experience. I was in my second year at the Art Academy, when at our Architectural Graphics class we were given the task to make architectural graphics of a baluster and the work had to be submitted the next day. All of us in the group stayed up the whole night at the Academy pulling sheets over sketch-boards, drying watercolour, coat after coat, with hair-dryers that we brought from home, in order to speed up the process. Eventually, we were on time and got our credits, but that took us a whole night of hard work without a minute of sleep. I wish we had markers in those days!

Of course, markers may not have been the best choice for doing a baluster on an A2 leaf (594 x 420 mm or 23.4 x 16.5 in), but I want you to see the point I am trying to make. What is the aim of an architectural drawing? To cultivate a sense of beauty, to start seeing fine aspects of the technique, to learn how to apply shadows, to acquire academic expertise of delivering architectural projects. Today, I think, all of these practical skills could have been acquired using a smaller A4 format and markers, while saving enormous amount of time.

I adore and hold in highest regard the technique of classical architectural graphics. Moreover, I very much like the process itself: when you rub a stick of Chinese ink on a glass, and fill plenty of pots with different tones of the ink: from the one with the highest concentration, almost black, to stone grey. At such moments I really feel the connection with the beautiful ancient technique that the great old masters possessed.

It is great if you have plenty of time to practice academic skills. Indeed, during the years at the Academy, it was meaningful and important. However let us look at it from a designer's point of view: it would be great to spend unlimited time and funds on a project or training, but the fact of life is that we have to do more in less time. With all the love for architectural graphics, everyone would agree that spending 8 hours on a baluster watercolour is a bit too much. On the other hand, markers are a very quick and effective tool. From my personal experience I can see how much faster the development of a project moves along with them, and most importantly, they are a source of much joy and satisfaction. It is my number one choice for interior sketching. I would like to talk about them in a little more detail.

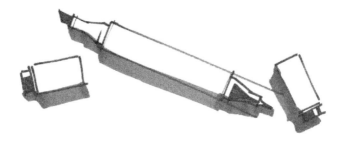

# **3.2.** Distinctive qualities of markers

Markers are a very exciting material which falls somewhere in between graphic and painting techniques combining the best features of both. It is a kind of a 'universal soldier'. From the watercolour it borrows its most beautiful feature of semi-transparency which fills a work with lightness and air. From graphic tools (such as coloured pencils) it borrows precision of drawing and hatching – you know exactly the way the tip of a marker will go and how the hatching will cover the space. Therefore markers enable us to create textures and tone gradations. A marker usually has two tips (sometimes even three): a thin and a wide one. Alternatively there's also a brush-tip, which is my absolute favourite.

It is interesting to compare marker and watercolour techniques. Even if you are a beginner, your first sketch with markers will be a success, whereas with watercolour this may not be the case. Why is that? The thing is when you take paint with a brush and add water, the result can be unpredictable, as you must feel the proportions of paint and water. Watercolour is considered to be the most intricate technique among artists, which is why you may not succeed at first unless you have a natural talent or penchant for this technique. Even though it is a classical technique for architectural renderings, almost all Art Academies and Schools of Architecture teach their students this technique. It does not let you attain the same speed, spontaneity and lightness of performance as markers do. My advice for beginners is this: use markers, and when you become familiar with this material, when you have understood the main principles and techniques, that's when you can start using watercolour, pastel and any other technique. For me, watercolour has always been one of my favourite techniques, even since my art school days, but now I mostly use it for landscapes, urban sketches, whereas for interior sketches, where high speed of performance is of great importance, I almost always opt for markers.

Markers palette consists of very beautiful pure colours, which wonderfully superimpose on top of one another creating even more admirable and intricate tones. Their semi-transparency lets you do tone gradations and beautiful texture effects. The possibility to create smooth gradations, the rich colour palette, and the ease of mastering – all these things have made markers the number one material with many designers.

Example of my Stylefile markers palette:

600
Turquoise Blue

306
Powder Pink

112
Cream

116
Walnut

800
Burnt Sienna

802
Bronze

816
Natural Oak

900
Black

216
Orange

372
Wine Red

522
Prussian Blue

WG 3
Warm Grey 3

NG4
Neutral Grey 4

# 3.3. Tips on materials

## How did it all begin?

It all started in Asia, in Japan. I think, the most popular marker brand today is Copic, and they are made in Japan. At first, they were used to draw comics, anime, and, as far as the tone is concerned, they were predominantly bright or skin coloured. Then this remarkable material was noticed by industrial designers and, industrial sketching rapidly evolved into a whole new art form. Today industrial design and markers are inseparable. Type 'industrial sketching' in the YouTube's search box and you will get a huge list of links to lessons for both beginners and professionals on how to use markers. Professionals who are great at drawing cars, machine parts and various consumer products (from tooth brushes to vacuum cleaners) are very popular and are in high demand.

Subsequently, this 'marker trend' has been picked up by architects and interior designers and a new profession has emerged: visualizer or, rather, hand-renderer, a person who does visualisations for a project. Copic manufacturers understood these trends too and today Copic palette includes hundreds of colours. For example, Copic grey colour comes in 40 different shades!

That's how the sketching wave began rolling from Asia and now has overwhelmed Europe, Russia and America. Now that initial excitement about the computer techniques has died out and people can see clearly there is a renewed interest in free hand drawing.

# History

I remember my impulse purchase at an Art supplies shop: it was only two colours Promarker Vanilla and Copic No. 6 Neutral Grey. I just took to the idea of two tips (professional markers usually have two tips: at one side it is a spatula tip, and at the other, it is a thin one), as it is quite convenient when you have to fill with colour larger spaces and then add detail. Buying markers for the first time, I was not at all intending to make the shift: I was fully satisfied with coloured pencils and watercolour. However, when I tried them in one of my project drawings, I understood that this was my ideal technique! I liked the way they glided on paper, their great quality of semi-transparency, a brilliant colour palette and how I was able to create amazing effects of tone and gradient – all this made me realise the superiority of markers over other materials.

Of course, the quality of material will influence the result. For example, if you ever tried watercolours and starting with cheap synthetic brushes, substandard paper and cheap watercolours, then the outcome must have looked accordingly. It is the same with markers. Good quality professional tools will instantly provide you with excellent result - even your first sketch will be a success! Markers do cost a pretty sum but this is an investment worth every penny!

## Which colours?

First and foremost, buy basic colours, as you will need them most. For interior sketching, it is better not to use pure, bright colours, but a bit 'dusty', 'noble' tones. What does it mean? With interiors it is better to choose colours that people would feel comfortable to live in. A typical palette would include beige and grey, blue, olive, and woody tones.

You can buy markers individually or in sets. There are even sets of ready-to-go colour combinations for architects and designers which consist of marker colours that work well with one another.

# You first marker selection might be as follows:

◆ Light gray (NG 2, Neutral Grey #2)

◆ Mid-gray (NG 4)

◆ Dark gray (NG 7)

◆ Light beige (or vanilla)

◆ Olive

◆ Dark brown (chocolate)

◆ Black

As you can see, there are seven colours all in all, of which three are grey shades. Greys holds a special place in interior sketching. They are used in the first place given a background colour to the entire sketch. Grey markers differ not only in tone, but also in warmth and coldness: there are Neutral Greys, Cool Greys and Warm Greys. To start with, you will need Neutral Greys. Usually they are marked by 'N' with a number: the higher the number, the darker the tone.

## What brand of markers to buy?

One of the first questions people ask in my online sketching classes is about materials. What brand of markers is the best? How various brand of markers differ from one another?

Up until now, I have tested 4 brands: Promarker, Copic, Stylefile marker and Chartpak. All of them are good. These firms make professional quality markers that are perfect for drawing and are non toxic.

If I was to pick my favourite, it would be Copic. They have an extremely wide array not only of colours but also of marker tips. These include 'Classic' markers, 'Extra Wide' ones, the thin 'Ciao' markers and remarkable 'Sketch' (the last two have brush points). Maybe it is Copic Ciao that has influenced my technique most of all. Firstly, they have a thin body that is very convenient to hold in hand. However, the main difference is that at one side there is a wide tip (incidentally, a bit narrower than a Copic Sketch, Promarker or Stylefile), and at the other end there is a brush tip, also known as the 'super brush'. Which truly leaves up to its name! It is the brush that lets you make absolutely photo-realistic effects and fantastic not only for sketching but also for landscape drawings, abstract painting, portraits, architectural sketches and even for calligraphy. Copic markers can be refilled and that is their tremendous advantage over other brands. Although they are the most expensive markers available, in the long term Copics are the more cost-efficient.

Promarker is also very good. They are very similar to Stylefile and Copic Classic. But these are single-use markers, which cannot be refilled.

Chartpak is markedly different from the markers mentioned above. These markers have one very wide tip, that is highly convenient for interior sketching. The only disadvantage is that these markers have a rather strong smell of solvent.

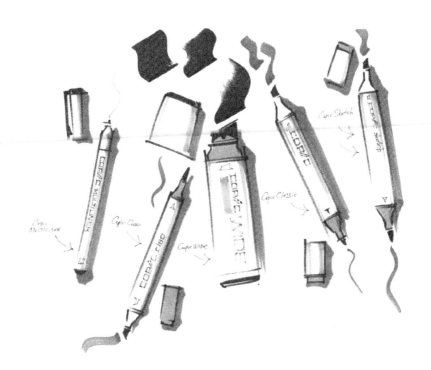

# A couple more tips

- Before buying a marker, test it in the art supplies shop and find a marker that suits you best. If you don't have such an opportunity, watch videos on marker brands on YouTube – this will help you make a decision about which materials are most suitable for you.

- When you realize that sketching is 'your thing', be ready to invest into quality materials, training courses and books. This way you can develop your skill to become very good at sketching. This will happen quite fast. Sketching will be of great use in your work and will raise your professional skills level.

- Probably it is better to buy markers in sets, because when you buy them individually at an art supplies shop, they are often already half empty as too many people test them.

- It is recommended that you keep markers horizontally – this will extend their service life.

- Storage and transportation: keep your markers away from the sun. If you are going on a trip, pack them into a hand-carried baggage, because the low temperatures in the baggage compartment will have adverse effect on the pigments inside the markers.

# Paper for markers

A lot depends on the special paper manufactured specifically for markers. I would like to share my own experience: at first I used ordinary cartridge A4 paper, before I noticed that markers bled right through and my markers ran out of ink very quickly. Eventually I discovered specialized bleed proof paper and my markers began to serve a lot longer.

I have used various brands such as Canson, Marker PAD, Creas and Stylefile. I have not found much difference between them. Perhaps Canson has a surface that is little whiter and silkier. It is important that your paper should have 70 g/m2 density, because if it is any lower, markers can behave unpredictably – they start leaking, cover the page in strips and streaks. What is the main advantage of this paper? It allows you to save plenty of material, because its reverse side is covered with special coating that repels excessive paint thus saving the marker ink. Only one side of this paper is actually intended for drawing. Also, colours look richer and deeper on such paper than on ordinary cartridge paper.

I would also advise you to buy a sketchbook or a pad so you can regularly practice even on the go. In the art of sketching consistency and everyday practice are of great importance. A sketch-book will allow you to keep practicing sketches any time and any place: during trips, in a traffic jam, in an airplane, or when you simply have 5-10 minutes of free time. Let the motto "not a day without drawing" be your companion.

## A few more helpful tips

Apart from the markers, you will also need a small set of additional materials which will enable you to fine-tune details and apply special effects and textures on your drawings. First and foremost, I must mention 3 types of white pens. They are:

1. A white crayon (I often use one by Faber-Castell)

2. White pastel crayon (Caran d'Ache)

3. And white jel pen

Each of these pens has a different covering density: the white crayon lets the marker colour be seen from underneath it, the pastel crayon has greater density, that of a chalk, and the jet pen allows you to make opaque white hatchings. The pen also comes handy in correcting mistakes on sketch plans, to convey effects of varnish, flecks of light, as well as shiny textures of materials such as glass and polished stone.

Secondly, you also can not do sketching without liners (e.g.: Copic, Faber-Castell) or permanent black pens: their thin tips will let you work over details and highlight key elements.

Don't be scared by the fact that there seems to be so many materials that you will need. I made a point to give you the whole list of materials that I use. Remember, to begin with, we only need 7 colours of markers, paper, a pencil and an eraser.

**The main thing is to start somewhere, and as you go along, you will realize what materials you enjoy and find most helpful.**

Having reached the end of this chapter, I would like to point out that sketching never stays still and is constantly evolving. New materials continue to emerge and they are ever more efficient and easy-to-use. If today there are already markers with three tips available, it would be interesting to hypothesize what comes next. So keep you eyes open, be curious and keep trying new things. Let us sum up:

# Minimum set

- Marker PAD paper (70 g/m2)

- Light grey marker (NG 2) marker

- Mid-grey (NG 4) marker

- Dark grey (NG 7) marker

- Light beige (or vanilla) marker

- Olive marker

- Dark brown (chocolate) marker

- Black marker

- A pencil

- An eraser

# More complete set might be as follows

◆ Marker PAD paper and a sketch book

◆ Copic kit of 36 or 72 colours

◆ White crayon

◆ White pastel pencil

◆ White jel pen

◆ Liners black and sepia (Copic multiliner or Faber-Castell,

thickness 0,3 or 0,5)

◆ A pencil

◆ An eraser

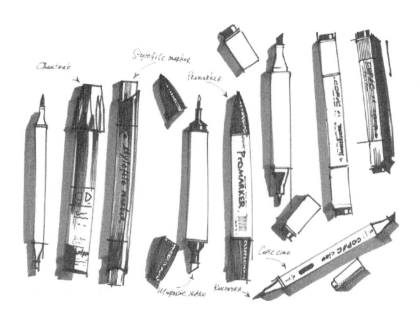

# PERSPECTIVE

## 04

In this chapter we will familiarize ourselves with the most extraordinary and most exciting field of descriptive geometry and will discover different types of perspective – the most important skill in interior sketching

# Ψ.). Fundamentals

Perspective is an area of descriptive geometry. Not many people are keen on learning descriptive geometry at school and for many it is synonymous with boring technical tasks and dull routine. Perhaps, some of you will even feel like skipping this chapter. Please don't! Perspective is an intriguing subject, full of surprising secrets and is absolutely essential for designers. It is this knowledge that will let you work wonders on paper allowing you to create exciting views of interiors and to reflect your ideas in the most effective way.

Perspective is the basic and most fundamental knowledge for sketching. It will help you deliver your projects expertly. Without it you will get nowhere – if you don't know the laws of perspective, then you lack the foundations, which means you cannot move on, and no rendering technique or stylistic device will help you out, if you don't have a clear understanding of how to plot a space. The eye of a man has an admirable organization and it is thanks to the laws of geometry, that we can put down on paper or visualize the real world in the way our brain perceives it.

**What types of perspective are there and which ones are of greatest importance to interior sketching?**

There are many types of perspective. To name but a few: aerial perspective, frontal perspective (or 1-point perspective), angular perspective (or 2-points perspective or oblique view), perspectives with 3, 4, 5 and even 6 vanishing points. So, which ones are of the greatest value to interior designers? First of all, it is the frontal perspective (it is sometimes called a perspective with one vanishing point), secondly, there is oblique view or angular perspective (with two vanishing points) and, finally, aerial perspective (or tonal perspective). If the first two allow us to correctly draw an interior, the last one will enable you to fill your drawing with air and convey three-dimensionality of space. We will take a closer look at the aerial perspective later in the book.

Once we master the basics, we can address more complex types of combined perspective – with three vanishing points, and various three-dimensional effects. These are exciting perspective techniques which add more expression to a drawing.

There is one artist that I want to point your attention to whose mastery of perspective I particularly admire.

■■■■■■■■■■■■■■■■■■■■■■■■■■■■■■■■■■■■■■■■■■■■■■■■■■■■■

*We adore chaos because we love to produce order.*
*Maurits Cornelis Escher*

■■■■■■■■■■■■■■■■■■■■■■■■■■■■■■■■■■■■■■■■■■■■■■■■■■■■■

I am talking about Dutch graphic artist Maurits C. Escher. His work is simply mind-boggling! My favourite work is his extraordinary self-portrait (you will find it on the Internet): he is drawing himself while looking in the mirror sphere which also reflects the interior. If you remove the ball, the room appears in 1-point perspective, but because the room is reflected in the spherical mirror surface of the ball, it causes amazing effects and distortions of the space. Escher's art is one of the brightest examples of mathematical laws of perspective coupled with the author's imagination. Escher published a book, "Impossible Worlds", where he plays with geometric laws, planes, creating inconceivable spaces. Scientists are well-versed in the beauty of mathematics and Escher shows all of us that beauty.

Once you grasp the rules of construction of geometry of a space, you can start experimenting with them. I call it 'playing with perspective'. All sketching masters have excellent command of this knowledge. So let's get going and discover it for ourselves!

# **4.2** 1-Point Perspective

We are forever indebted for this knowledge to the Italian Renaissance. In the second half of the XV-th century, Renaissance artists and mathematicians developed the linear perspective theory and brought precision and mathematics into mainstream art. Viva Italia!

Before that, artists drew 'by eye' or used Inverted Perspective, which is an art form unique to pre-renaissance religious art and is full of embedded meaning. As an example, look at Andrey Rublev's "Trinity" and observe how the space appears flat and converges towards the viewer.

Thanks to Renaissance and its masters, who were not only prolific artists, sculptors, architects, but also prodigious mathematicians, the laws of perspective were discovered. Brunelleschi, Alberti, Masaccio, Ghiberti, Piero della Francesca introduced the use of perspective, and, in doing so, forever changed further development of art.

Renaissance masters were so fluent in the complexities of geometric construction that they were able to apply their knowledge of perspective to perform most complicated tasks and solve quite challenging problems. For example, painting of a ceiling of a dome, has to take into account a variety of factors: first, people look at frescos from below, which significantly alters their perception. They also had to take into account the curved shape of the dome and correct for distortions that arise. Apart from that, there is a host of technical aspects such as erection of scaffolding, working at a high altitude, temperature, humidity (in the case of frescos, the humidity is very high, as painting is performed over damp plaster), technique of mixing colours, a problem of lighting, and even the position of a painter's body (for instance, Michelangelo almost completely lost his sight, while painting the Sistine Chapel).

In the 1-point perspective, we have a vanishing point, which is always on the horizon line. This vanishing point is where all the lines converge to (that's why it is

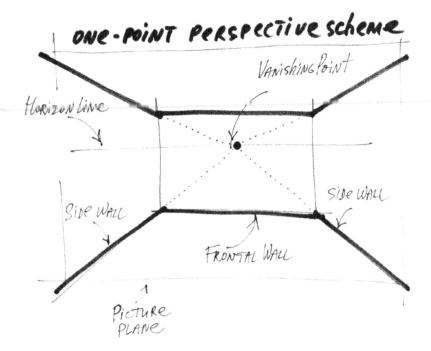

**one-point perspective scheme**

Vanishing Point

Horizon Line

Side Wall

Side Wall

Frontal Wall

Picture Plane

called 1-point perspective). When we draw an interior, we see three walls: one that is parallel to the picture plane (frontal wall) and two side walls.

## When should we use 1-point perspective?

1-point perspective is an ideal choice for depicting public spaces: bars, cafes, restaurants, hotel lobbies, as well as spacious residential interiors: sitting rooms, dining rooms, halls and lounges, etc. This view lets you represent your idea on a drawing by showing the maximum amount of space. Suppose, we have a restaurant layout, rectangular in shape: it would be sufficient to draw two 1-point perspective views – in one direction as you enter and one in the reverse. If we were to use a 2-point perspective view to demonstrate the design idea, we would have to draw all four corners of the space, plus a general view, a view from above, or even make a model (at least 5 sketches in total). In contrast, the 1-point perspective view allows you to show the idea with only two drawings.

We can change the position of the vanishing point in relation to the centre of the picture plane placing it anywhere on the horizon line. It can be right in the centre, or it can be shifted to the right or to the left. This will make the picture asymmetric. This adds dynamism to the composition and allows you to reveal one of the walls to a greater extent. However, when the vanishing point is right in the centre, both walls are shown to the same degree, and, thus, appear balanced. In fact, it is this placement of the vanishing point that is often used in classical drawings of interiors. Classics loves symmetry.

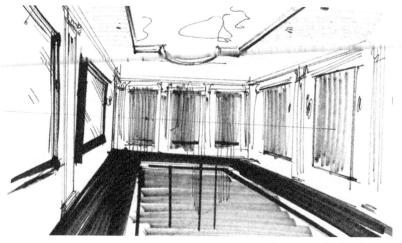

My drawing of an interior in
1-point perspective

# ४.३. 2-Points Perspective

Another type of perspective important for designers is the perspective with two vanishing points. It is often called an «Oblique View». In this view, horizon contains two vanishing points, and the picture reveals two walls of a space. You can move these points on the horizon line, but it is important that the distance between them should remain the same fixed value (usually this distance equals to the diagonal of the picture plane). When you have understood all the most important basic laws of perspective, you will be able to experiment with them, creating drawings with the most effective angles.

### In which case 2-points perspective is the best choice?

It is indispensable when we want to show a space containing one main object, a dominant feature. In the bedroom, it is a bed. In the study, it is a desk. In the nursery, it is a cot. And so on...

This perspective is ideal for small spaces, or when we want to draw in detail a specific corner of an interior. It is important that we draw this object in great detail. Also it is the oblique view that allows us to show furnishings and other separate objects. I often use it to specify upholstery. A picture is worth a thousand words and it is way easier to send an image along with an order for a piece of furniture depicting exactly what I had in mind.

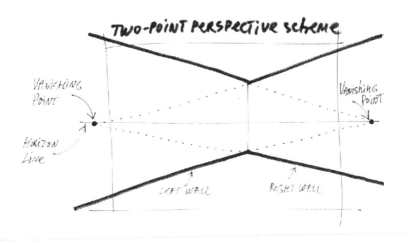

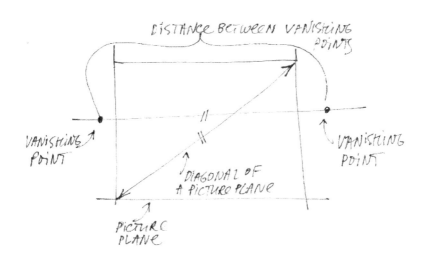

# ❧.❧. Combination of 1-Point and 2-Points Perspectives

It is also possible to combine the two kinds of perspective. For example, below there is a drawing of an interior created in 1-point perspective overall. However, observe how the two armchairs placed at an angle – they are done in 2-points perspective.

My drawing of an interior in 1-point perspective with armchairs done in 2-points perspective

# 4.5. Special effects

## Perspective with a high horizon line ('view from above')

A very interesting perspective for designers is a perspective with an artificially high eye level. A third vanishing point way down below, beyond borders of the picture, comes into view. This nuance is easily recognisable as the vertical lines of the walls that previously went parallel to each other as well as to the edges of the paper sheet are now no longer parallel and are converging at some point beyond the drawings. This is an advanced technique and this is what I call 'playing with perspective'.

### What is the main trick here?

We show an interior using an extremely high horizon line, our eye level is somewhere right underneath the ceiling as if we were looking at the room standing on a high step-ladder.

### What is the outcome of this technique and in which case this view is the best choice?

Because of the high horizon line, we get an exciting and effective angle view, which is ideal for drawing small spaces, such as a bathrooms or a small kitchens. This technique also comes very handy when, for instance, you want to show charming motifs on the floor.

It is easy to remember – the higher the horizon, the greater is the amount of the floor visible; the lower the horizon, the greater is the amount of the ceiling visible. For example, let's say you want to show pretty plaster work on the ceiling, all of this must be taken into account at the very first stages when planning a drawing.

# Combined perspective

This is probably my favourite way of constructing geometry of a space. An interior constructed in this way looks most impressive and usually to its greatest advantage.

As the name suggests, the construction principles of both the 2-points and the 1-point perspectives are combined in the same drawing. In my eCourse "PRO", I give a very detailed description of this interesting method of construction which I considered to be advanced and beyond the scope of this book.

## What other interesting techniques are there?

There is, for example, 'the fish eye effect' perspective when we see an interior as if we were looking through a photo camera lens producing a visual distortion of a wide panoramic or hemispherical image.

Sometimes using several horizon lines in one drawing makes for an interesting composition. It is possible also to use several vanishing points in 1-point perspective drawing. These are additional options which you can easily grasp once you have a good command of the basics.

# **4.6.** Aerial Perspective

There are two quite poetic, in my opinion, quotes about aerial perspective that come to mind.

The first was made by Leonardo da Vinci:

> *At long distances, objects seem ambiguous and opaque, and you must give them the same blurred look, otherwise they would look in your picture as if they were at the same distance. Don't give a clear outline to the objects that are far from your eyes, for at a distance not only these outlines but also some parts of objects become imperceptible. And the farthest objects, because of a great amount of air between your eyes and these objects, look blue, almost the colour of air.*

The second one is from a book by Italian Renaissance artist and architect Leon Battista Alberti "On Painting":

> *With long distance, objects and figures loose the force of colour, weaken.*

Aerial perspective is sometimes called a "tonal" perspective and it is of great use to designers. I will describe a simple and effective way of using it. To better understand aerial perspective we will need a bit of imagination. Imagine that the interior that you would like to draw is filled with heavy fog. You can see clearly the objects that are closer to you: you can clearly see details, see textures and colours. As the distance increases, objects become engulfed in white haze, as if they dissolve with distance.

Thus, we come to the notions of:

◆ Foreground

◆ Middleground

◆ Background

Foreground is that, which is the nearest to the observer; the middle ground is a little further from us; and finally, background is at the very end of the scene. Aerial perspective enables you to capture the air and the volume of a space, as if by magic a 3D picture emerges on a flat to dimensional page.

### What are the ways to convey aerial perspective on a drawing?

Let us see how the masters that we know go about it. You are already familiar with one method, the technique of Sergio Rodrigues (Chapter 2 "Masters"), of outlining objects in the foreground with a thicker and saturated line, and, drawing objects in the background in light, thin lines, although still in detail. This is an effective and expressive method, which is also very simple.

The second one is the classical technique: draw objects in the foreground carefully, showing their textures and detail, and draw a schematic outline of the background in faint lines. The principle is simple: the nearer, the more detailed and neat is the drawing; the further, the less detail and quieter, lighter, more restrained are the colours. It is important to understand that the greater the volume of air between our eyes and the objects, the more they get 'dissolved in the haze', as though losing their colour. There emerges the characteristic gradient: the greater the distance, the more faded objects become.

How does Richard Chadwick (Chapter 2 "Masters") deals with the aerial perspective? He applies a very interesting and unusual technique that I call "the contradiction trick". In almost all of his sketches it is in the centre of the drawing that gets more intense, dense colouring. In fact, Chadwick seems to be more involved with the background, while the foreground is left black-and-white. So, it is the other way round, a complete opposite of the classic approach: the background is more detailed and the foreground is left lighter and drawn only in lines. Despite this reversal, there is sense of air and space in his works. How then does he achieve that? Chadwick attains the effect of aerial perspective through detailed elaboration of textures and small objects in the foreground. For example, he often shows the textures of the floors (marble, wood, tiling motifs), as well as he uses black liner to neatly draw small objects in the foreground in great detail. Chadwick's favourite subject is interiors of bars, cafes and restaurants. Take a closer look at how he meticulously works over dozens of wine glasses in every detail in the foreground, or how he goes about the wood textures and tiling imperfections.

My copy of master's work

# **4.7. Summary**

In this chapter I have given a brief outline of the rich and diverse world of different types of perspective. The subject is extraordinarily interesting and profound, but the key thing is that these techniques can be applied practically. Once you have come to grips with fundamental concepts and principles of perspective, you can go on to explore the subject on your own, experiment, create incredible worlds of your own, like M. Escher's, play about with effects, bring together different perspectives in one drawing and achieve breathtaking results. The ability to apply these techniques will allow you to find the most winning methods of visualization of your projects and to present your ideas to your clients in the best possible light.

The fundamental thing is that you have to carry out analysis of your future drawing before you start constructing the perspective. In the first place, you must understand what is it that you want to show, and then decide on a perspective technique that will enable you to reach your goal in the best possible way. After that, you have to decide how high you want to place the horizon line. What is it that you want to reveal to the greatest extent? Would it be the ceiling or the floor? Which wall would you like to reveal more in your sketch? These are the main questions to ask yourself before you start drawing. These are the starting point of every drawing.

An excellent idea would be to do a couple of little drafts of a small format, say, 7 x 10 cm, to find the best position for vanishing points and find the best angle.

**Now that you have the knowledge, the ball is in your court – let's put it into practice!**

My drawing of an interior in
1-point perspective

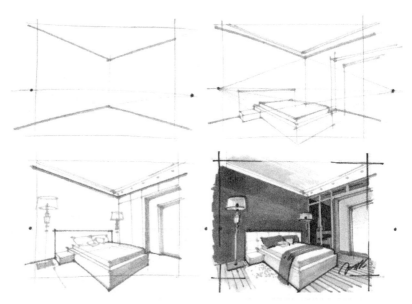

My process of drawing an interior
in 2-points perspective

# SKETCH-PLAN

## 05

This chapter will introduce you to the best way to start practicing interior sketching, and will provide you with a step-by-step guide to how to make a great sketch-plan

# 5.1. Layout plan with furnishings. Analysis.

In the preceding chapters we have analyzed the works of the masters, have learned many things about perspective, and have decided upon materials that we will need. Let us get down to practice. Let us start with one of the most significant things for an interior designer – a layout plan with furnishings. This is the start of any project, which contains a wealth of information and is the first bit of visual information that you put in front of a client.

### What is a layout plan?

Layout plan is a horizontal section, a view from above. As a rule, it is imagined as being made at a height of one meter above the floor. There are architects and designers who are completely enthralled by layouts, experiencing great aesthetic pleasure from producing elegant and functional plans. It is as if they are in that room, walking around it, experiencing every passage and corner in their thoughts. To tell the truth, I also adore examining plans. I particularly like inspecting plans of small flats and houses, keen to introduce interesting ideas and solutions.

The problem is that not all customers can "read drafts". For most people, a layout plan with a furniture arrangement looks rather sterile – a black and white printout of a projection in scale amidst a heap of working drawings.

Sketch-plan is something completely different. It is the «Bomb», let me tell you! You should have seen customers' faces when they are shown a plan drawn with markers. It all becomes quite clear to them all of a sudden. Particularly, you get the "wow-effect" when, at the same meeting, you also show them sketches of a prospective interior. Thanks to this creative approach, 'working drawings' (which sounds utterly boring to clients) are the most exciting things to work on and analyze! Interestingly many of my students initially think that a sketch plan could not be more boring. However, they soon discover that it could not be further from the truth and they end up spending many hours practicing this technique.

Creation of a sketch-plan is a very simple procedure. I suppose, that is the easiest and the most exciting part of interior sketching. I am sure you too will be able to master this new skill without much trouble!

Next, I will give a detailed step-by-step description of all stages of drawing of a sketch-plan with markers.

**Let's get down to practice! Let's rock!**

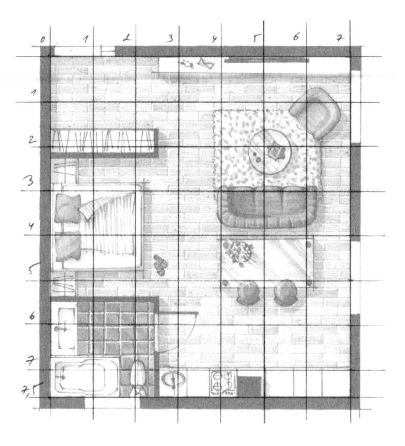

# 5.2. Step-by-step guide

We will start by drawing a sketch-plan of a small studio apartment where I will demonstrate all the steps that you will need to take. You will need an A4 sheet of marker paper, you can download the original plan from my website or by coping this from this book **(page# ??)**. There are two ways of doing it, if you are printing the plan, make sure that you put the marker paper appropriately, so that the plan prints on the right side of the paper. If you are tracing your plan by hand, marker paper is transparent enough to place over page **#73?** and copy the details. Sometimes, when I am short for time, I place a sheet of marker paper on my screen, fix it with masking tape and trace it by hand. Of course the best way is to have your plan to scale, however, for the purposes of this exercise the plan we are going to work on will not be to scale.

So now you have a plan of the space in front of you. The most important thing from here is introducing to your plan shadows which will give your drawing depths, greater clarity, readability and realism. In order to create shadows thrown by objects in your sketch plan, you must first decide position on the source of light in your room. Is it the natural light coming from the window? Or perhaps is it the electric chandelier complimented by a row of downlights along a wall? Or is it the traditional approach of strategically placing table lamps and picture lights in the room? To start off we will look at the classical case of light falling from the left at an angle of 45 degrees and therefore all shadows falling to the right of objects.

The list of steps required to create a successful sketch-plan is as follows:

**Shadows > Base > Textures> Details > Filling out layout details**

**Let's look at each step in detail.**

# Step 1: Shadows

With a mid-grey marker (Neutral Grey No. 3) draw shadows from objects and walls falling to the right of the objects. You will immediately get the effect of volume, and three-dimensionality.

You can help yourself by making preparatory guidelines in pencil by going at a 45 degrees angle from the objects and filling the ticked off areas with markers.

**This is the first and most important step, which should not be skipped, otherwise your sketch-plan is going to look like a colouring book as opposed to a professional project.**

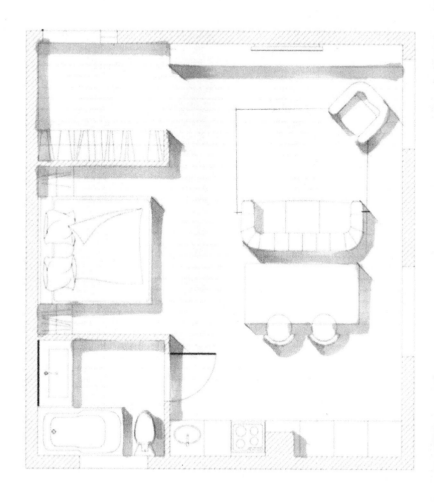

# Step 2: Basic colours for the flooring

This is the main, ground colour for our sketch-plan which will make it look tied together and coherent. First of all, fill with colour the flooring materials. Usually, it is wood, tiling or fitted carpet. Choose an appropriate colour and use the wider chamfered tip of the marker to colour the whole surface of the floor, including going over the shadows you placed on sketch-plan in Step 1. Lay the marker strokes in the direction the floor covering is laid (horizontally, vertically or diagonally).

**Tip**: if the flooring is made of light wood, then you should choose a lighter marker for your shadows in Step 1 (Neutral Grey No. 2), otherwise an overly strong contrast might appear between the shadow and the base, which will look crude, glaring and disjoined. If you have the flooring of dark wood and the shadows were made in light grey, the shadows will 'get lost', so go for a darker grey such as Neutral Grey No. 5. Find the optimal combination, you can experiment on a separate sheet of paper.

It is important to draw neatly, to put the colouring on the objects evenly, so as not to divert the attention of an observer.

**Remember that the ultimate purpose of a sketch-plan is to get across your ideas in a most vivid, attractive and exciting way.**

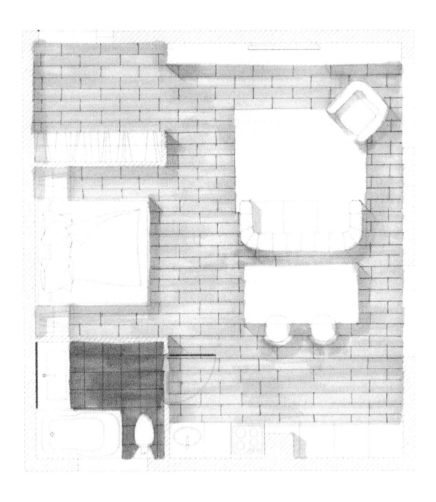

# Step 3: Detailing the parquet floor

After you have applied the base colour, you can add a few further layers of detail.

Let's take parquet for example.

Wood is a very beautiful and attractive material that is rich and varied with no two parquet pieces being the same. How can you render such complexity? Using the same marker as you used to fill the parquet base colour, go over selected pieces of parquet along each board, but chose your boards randomly so that some appear darker than the others. If you are short for time you can stop here; however, if time permits, elaborate on textures of selected pieces of parquet.

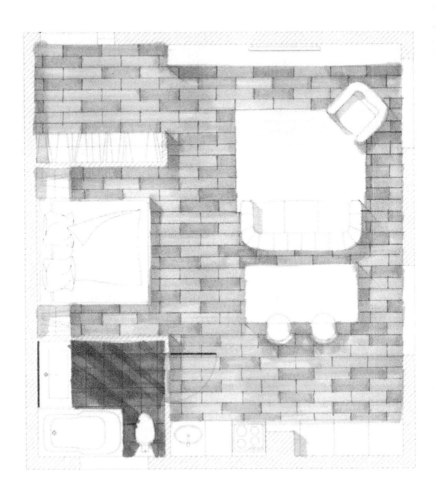

Some shy away from drawing annual rings characteristic of wood textures, but there is no magic to it, they are simply curvy horizontal lines in pencil. If you feel unsure try it first on a separate sheet of paper. Now that we have realistically looking wood, we can add further layers of realism by indicating how light falls on parquet boards. In accordance with the chosen source of light, using a white jel pen, pick up lightly corners of the parquet pieces.

The same applies to tiles – the texture application procedure is similar to that of the parquet. If you have glazed tiling, use the architects' favourite technique "ruler at 45 degrees": put a ruler at 45 degrees angle and make swift abrupt hatchings using the thin tip of a marker. Diagonal hatching make a beautiful "glistening effect". This trick can be used when you depict glass, mirror and any other reflective or polished surfaces.

After that divide the floor into separate tiles using a pencil or a black liner and indicate corners where the light hits the tiles with a white jel pen. As you can see both the parquet boards and tiles now look 3-dimensional.

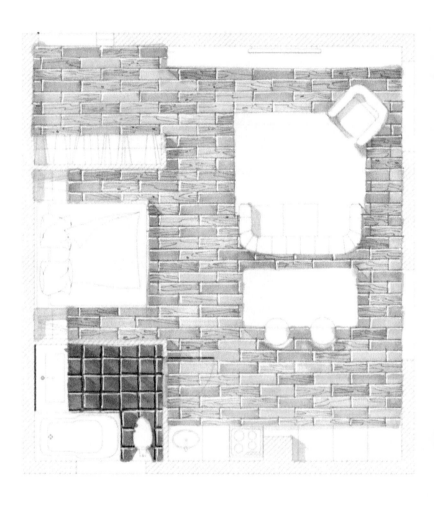

# Step 4: Adding objects and outlining

Let's move on to the objects. Fill the bed, arm-chair and chairs with their base colours.

Now the task is to apply colour on the drawing so that our sketch-plan would have white patches only in those places that are white in reality (for example, sanitary ware and bed sheets).

Apply small dots on the carpet with a tip of a marker with different amount of pressure!

Now every object on your drawing has its own particular colour. Notice how the carpet, the bed sheet and the glass tabletop now have their own textures. You can be as inventive and creative as you like at this stage, for example if your carpet or bed linen has an interesting pattern you can spend a few minutes drawing it. Please be aware that we are going to add a table in front of the sofa in the next step.

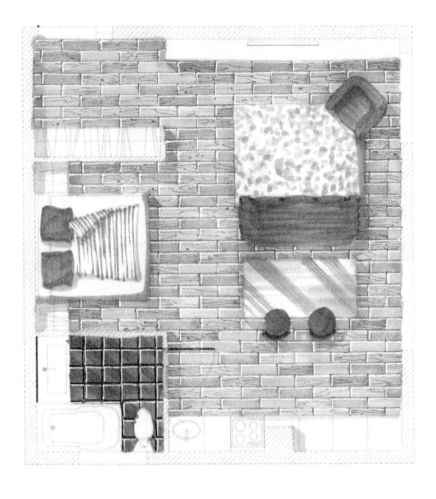

Then add **detail**: draw the linen, and other **"enlivenings"**, give volume to the bed and arm-chair using shadows.

Let us elaborate on the rug, doing flaky hatching, or just making a dotty surface to convey a napped texture.

**Glass surface**: notice how we used the ruler at 45 degrees method to render the table top. Remember that we have a table with a transparent glass top, so you could see the floor though it, that is why we should add a little flooring colouring into the surface of the table and make chairs that seat partially underneath table visible.

Add extra shadows with a thin tip to the sofa and armchair cushions, bed pillows, dining chairs.

**Outline technique**: with a black liner (0.3 thickness usually works well), go over the outlines of the objects in the room.

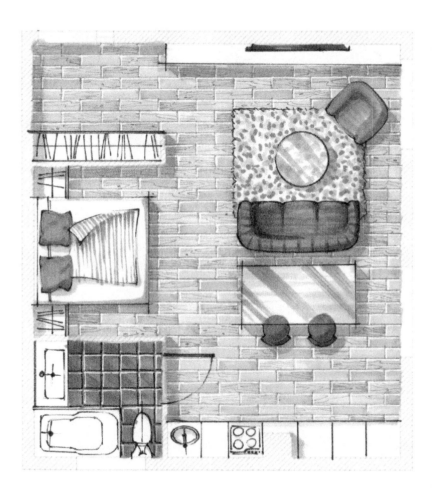

## Step 5: Walls and interior decoration

In most Schools of Architecture, students are taught to fill the walls on their plans with black Chinese ink. We shall use a black marker, which is a lot easier as Chinese ink often runs smearing all over the drawing.

First of all let us go over the outlines of the walls with a black liner (0.3 thickness) and then fill them in neatly with a black marker. It all starts looking remarkably attractive, doesn't it?

**Black walls work as a frame, as borders. They off set and accentuate all the other textures, shadows to a striking attractive effect.**

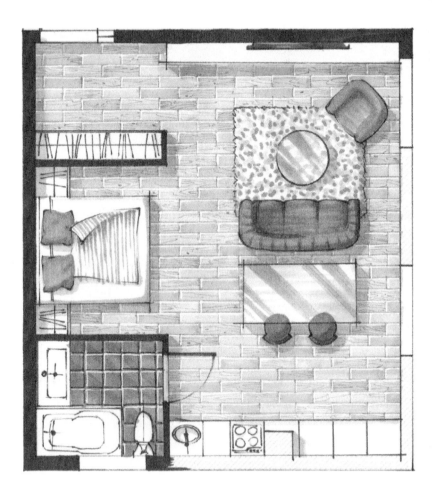

The last step would be to add a few final layout details and place a few further accents. Add every small detail and narrower shadows inside the objects. For example shadows on the back sink, bath and kitchen sink. We may also embellish our plan by adding books lying on the table, a bunch of flowers and a few other little things, what I call **"enlivenings"**.

**Congratulations! Your sketch-plan is finished!**

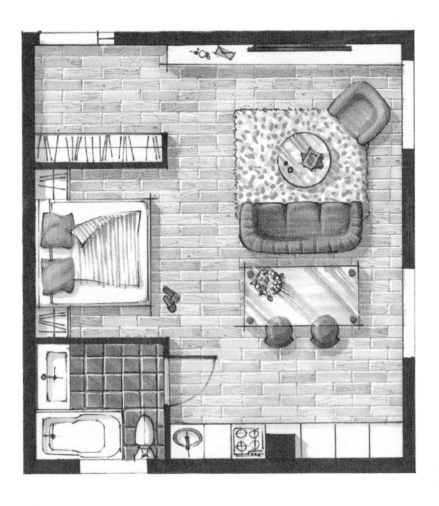

# The SKETCH

**06**
In this chapter we will discuss the key principles of drawing from a sketch-plan, discover the intricacies of 1-point perspective and draw our first perspective

# *6.).* Analysis

Now we are moving on to the very important subject of 1-point perspective practice, which I think is the number one skill for an interior designer. There are several methods to construct a 1-point perspective, but in this book I will describe one of the easiest, but most effective ones.

In this chapter, I will show you how you approach any project. As you may remember from the chapter on Perspective, before you start your sketch, it is very important to do preparatory analysis of your space and develop some initial ideas and concepts.

In this exercise, we will draw a 1-point perspective view from the sketch-plan that we just completed. We are going to do it in 1:100 scale and our drawing will be quite small. The main thing is to understand the principles of 'construction' a drawing and the sequence of steps.

Let's formulate the task. So, we have a studio apartment; total floor area 53 m2; room size 7m x 7, 5 m; ceiling height 3 m.

The question is how can we show the interior in the most advantageous way so that the customer be able to see and easily understand the idea and would be prepared to go ahead and pay for it?

In our case, to show the volume of the space to the maximum extent, we should stand near the kitchen counter and look towards the wall opposite, where the TV stands. And we should stand a bit closer to the window on the right hand side. Why choosing this particular location is important? This will allow the vanishing point to be shifted from the centre of the TV wall towards the right, which in term will show the left hand side wall with the bed against it a little bit more. This is exactly what we need! This will allow us to show the room to a greater extend, including the sofa and the bed.

**Solution**:

First of all let's draw grid on a plan with squares equal to 1 m in scale each (scale 1:100). You can use thin pencil or liner.

**Now let's move on to the sketch itself!**

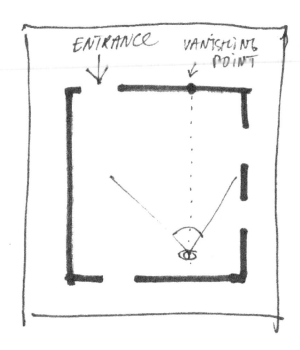

# 6.2. Step-by-step procedure

**Fig. 1:** Let's draw a picture plane on a horizontally placed A4 sheet of paper (210 x 297 mm 11.7 "x 8.3 ").

We shall use a **1:50 scale** one of the most commonly used in interior sketching, which means 1 m in reality corresponds to 2 cm on paper. Start by drawing a simple rectangle 6 cm by 14 cm: the height of ceiling is 3 m, so in our scale it translates to 6 cm; the length of the space is 7 m, so it will be 14 cm on our drawing.

Now, we are going to draw a **metric ruler** on our drawing plane by ticking off 2 cm intervals and then numbering them, vertically as well as horisontally.

**Fig. 2:** Now we are going to place line of horizon (eye level), which is an absolutely critical stage. In most cases, it is placed a little higher than the centre of the drawing. Why is that? In our situation, it is better to reveal the floor a little bit more, otherwise the table will block out the sofa completely. Let us place the eye level at 170 cm high of the floor (3.5 cm in scale). If instead we wanted to show a ceiling feature in our drawing such as a chandelier interesting plaster work or even a view of staircase balustrade on an upper level, we would place our horizon line lower than the centre of the drawing. In sketches of masters we most often come across three common heights for the eye level: 150, 160 and 170 cm from the floor level.

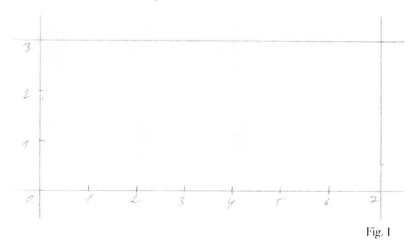

Fig. 1

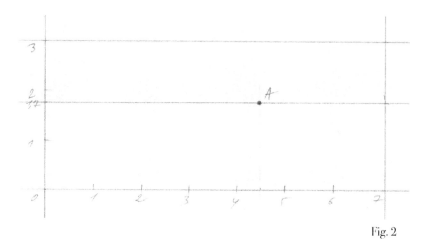

Fig. 2

Now we let's position **the vanishing point, and let's call it point A**. It is not without a reason that we chose to stand nearer to the window, since the more towards the right we place our vanishing point on the horizon line, the more of the left wall, where we have the bed, will be revealed. And the other way round: if we placed the vanishing point to the left, the more of the features on the right, such as the sofa, the armchair and the table would be revealed. So make sure that your vanishing point is located at 4,5 m horizontally and 1,7 meters vertically.

Fig. 3: Now, we are going to draw lines starting from each corner of picture plane and ending at the vanishing point. We say that the lines are converging to vanishing point.

Fig. 4: Let's measure one third of the picture plane dimensions and draw a **rectangle of the back wall**. In fact, you can take any height of the wall to your liking. But the choice that looks best is one third of the height of the picture plane.

**The geometry of the space is now finished! Well done!**

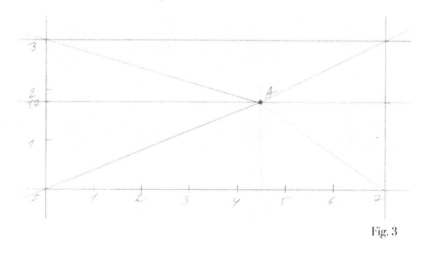

Fig. 3

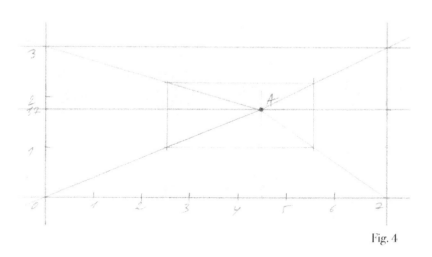

Fig. 4

The next step is to arrange furniture in our space by creating **geometry of the objects**. We will use precise method to do this properly. Let's draw a grid on the floor with 1 meter marks. This meter grid on the floor will allow us to place objects in the room precisely as well as to indicate their sizes furley accurately.

**Fig. 5:** From each mark we will now draw a line converging to point A.

**Fig. 6:** Let's draw a diagonal line through the 7th meter mark on the right edge of the drawing and the zero mark on the opposite wall. The line that extends will meet the Horizon Line at a point called **the Distance Point**.

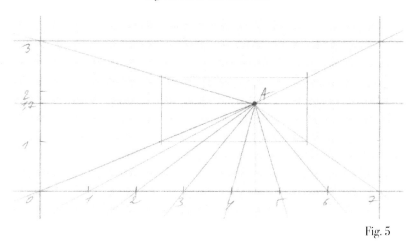

Fig. 5

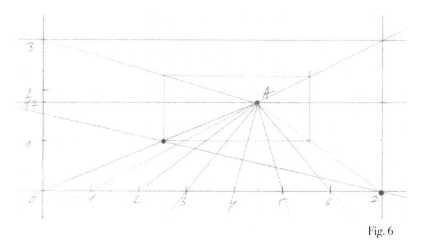

Fig. 6

**Fig. 7:** This line have crossed all the lines converging to point A we have previously drawn. Let's draw parallel lines through these points of intersection.

Notice how we now have the back wall, left and right walls, ceiling and in addition, the floor plane is split in 1 m square chunks.

Now that we have the grid on the floor, we can move on to arranging the furniture by creating geometry of the objects.

**Fig. 8:** Now we are going to depict the projections of furniture on the floor. First, let's show the main items: let us look at our sketch plan to determine what objects are situated in what positions. We'll do a bit of approximation in doing so to make our job easy.

**The bed** (2 m x 2 m) occupies the position from meter 3 to meter 5 (along the left wall) and from meter 0 to meter 2 (along the floor, projecting into the room). The **sofa** and the **table** are positioned opposite the bed at a distance of about two meters. Let's indicate their projections as well. Notice how the bed on the plan is positioned quite at 3-5 m along the left wall and extends slightly more than 2 metes into the room, however, for the purposes of interior sketching our approximation is perfectly acceptable.

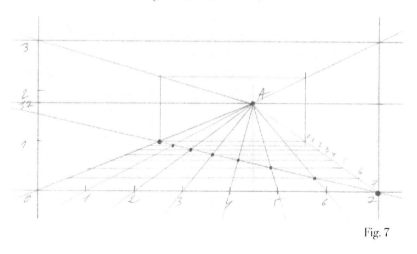

Fig. 7

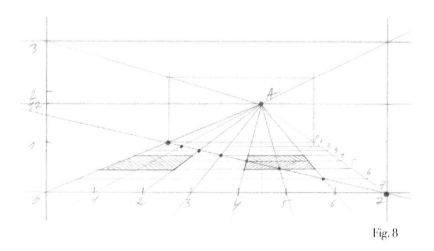

Fig. 8

**Fig. 9:** Then, let's show the internal partitions: the back of the wardrobe and the bathroom wall. The back of the wardrobe stands approximately at 2 m mark and is slightly longer than the bed. Let us show its footprint on the floor and extend the line up vertically where it meets the wall and across the ceiling.

**Fig. 10:** The second internal wall separates the bathroom from the rest of the studio. It starts somewhere between the 5th and the 6th meter along the left hand side wall. The process is similar to what we just did with the back of the wardrobe. However, in this case, we must also indicate the depts of the wall extending toward us. Always remember, in interior sketching vertical lines are always vertical, horizontal lines are always parallel to each other and all other lines converge to the vanishing point, point A. Let us draw the lines on the wall and the ceiling. This means, that we extend an imaginary (dotted line on the drawing) line from point A to point F and leave only the part we actually need.

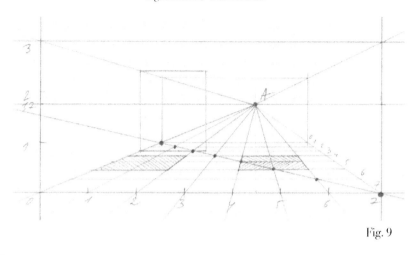

Fig. 9

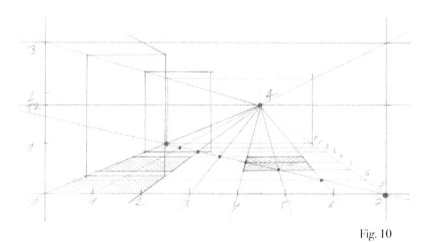

Fig. 10

**Fig. 11:** Now let's erect the heights of the furniture. The bed is 50 cm high, and the headboard is 1 meter hight from the floor. Mark those measurements on our vertical axis. Let us erect vertical lines from all four points of the footprint on the floor and build a box which is the wireframe of the bed.

**Fig. 12:** Let's use a slightly different procedure to build a box of the sofa is the wireframe of our **sofa**. In fact, we can only see the back of the sofa and also it is standing inside the room, away from the left and right handside walls. It was easier with the bed because it was against the wall and we could use our measuring scale to deduce its height. In this case, we need to find a supporting point by drawing the vertical on the picture plane at 4 m horizontally and 1 m vertically (Point D on the picture).

**Now that we have identified 1 m hight level we can draw a line converging to point A and find where that line crosses the vertical which forms the wireframe of our sofa. Always remember that all the measurement of heights happens against our ruler, on the picture plane.**

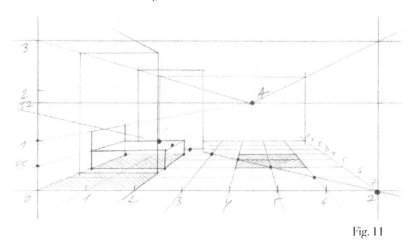

Fig. 11

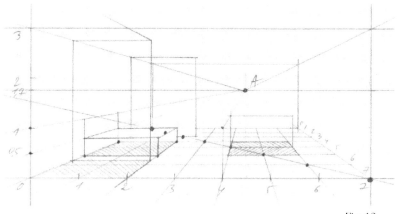

Fig. 12

**Fig. 13:** Let us figure out the **table**. The height is 70 cm this time (1.5 cm on our scale). Let us measure this height on the same supporting perpendicular line that we used for the sofa's and project that height by drawing a line between our measured height and point A and finding where that line intersects the perpendicular rising from the corner of the table.

**Fig. 14:** Let us go over the outlines of the objects with a pen. Let us show the **windows**. The window sill height in reality is 70 cm (1.5 cm in scale); the window itself is 2 m height in reality.

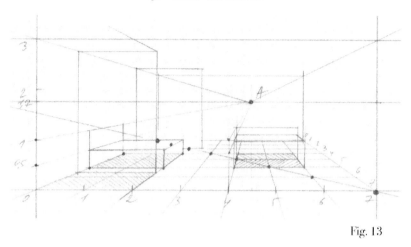

Fig. 13

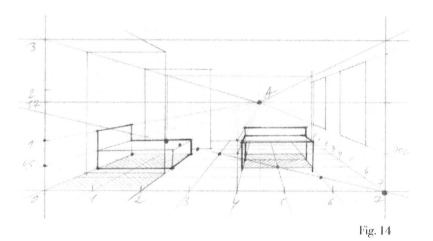

Fig. 14

**Fig. 15:** It is now time to sort things out with the **aerial perspective** in our sketch.

It is time to deal with the foreground and background. Let us accentuate the foreground with thicker lines (remember the chapter Masters and S. Rodrigues), and after doing that, elaborate on the partitions, and emphasize the geometry of the space.

**Note**: Although the bed is behind the partition, do go over its outlines – it is a very interesting stylistic device.

Now accentuate the graphics of the space by emphasizing walls.

**Fig. 16:** Let us add a bit of tone and the **glass effect** that we have already learned in Chapter 5 (ruler at 45 degrees). I'm depicting the wall of the bathroom as made of glass, but it equally can be shown as solid.

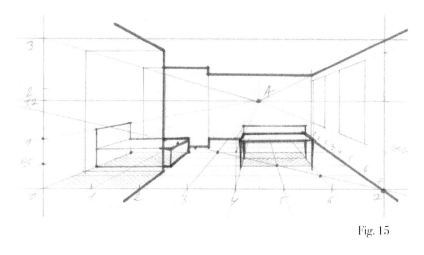

Fig. 15

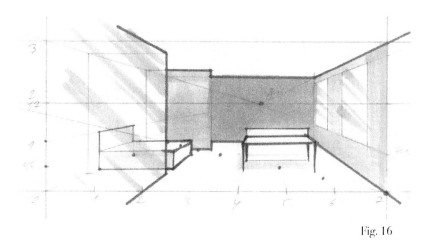

Fig. 16

**Fig. 17:** Add a little more detail freehand, such as lamps, accessories, and all the **"enlivenings"**.

Add borders and your signature. And here you are! Your first sketch drawn from a plan is finished.

### Congratulations!

**We have tested all the basic skills of sketching. It is up to you to practice and develop them further.**

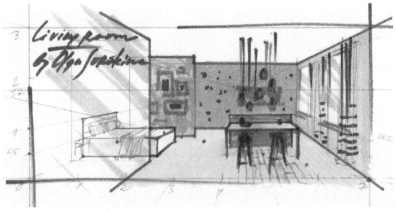

Fig. 17

# TECHNIQUES

## 07

This chapter will tell you about interesting techniques combining computer and freehand drawing, about creation of hybrid sketches, and about blending different techniques in general

# 7.1. Experiments

Sketching gives you an exciting opportunity to experiment with materials. For example, you can do an interior using watercolours and markers at the same time. In fact, one can use a very unusual but common material that everyone has at home.

In my sketch of the Noma restaurant in Copenhagen, I used only a few colours: a couple of watercolour tones, three markers (black, vanilla and brown) and... salt to render an interesting texture of wood.

## Procedure

I sprinkled a little salt on a still wet watercolour. The excess of paint was absorbed by the salt. After all of it dried up, it made a lovely uneven texture. Then I went on to add furniture and accentuated everything with markers. And here you are!

You can also combine colour pencils with pastel. Don't be afraid to experiment: there is no pressure – it is only a drawing! However, the result may surpass your expectations.

# 7.2. Hybrid sketches

When you use a computer or a graphics tablet, keep in mind that the key thing is synergy between new technologies and freehand mastery. I must admit, I actually removed 3D Max from my computer, but I still enjoy working in AutoCAD, Corel and Photoshop.

Computer graphics and freehand drawing can get along wonderfully and complement each other. Some of the modern artists work are equally good at both techniques, creating the so called **hybrids** making the most of computer capabilities and freehand charm (for example, Michelle Morelan).

How do you go about it? I will now tell you about it in a bit more detail, as I was using this technique when I was working as a designer for various companies. This technique is indispensable if you have to submit the project urgently but 3D renders have not been finished yet.

# Hybrid technique: a step-by-step procedure

1. Make a box of a room with all the window and door openings or simply import your AutoCAD layout of the room into 3D Max and extrude the walls (lift up the height).

2. Fill the scene with boxes (the simplest shape in 3D Max) according to the sizes of the furniture, and position them in accordance with your plan.

3. Set up the camera, find a good view angle and render the scene.

4. Having finished rendering, you can print it out and draw over it, or transfer the perspective view and the outlines of objects onto paper and use markers to "refine details and textures". You can also scan the completed sketch and bring it to perfection in Adobe Photoshop.

The best thing about this technique is that you don't have to manually construct the geometry of the space and the objects which reduces the time required by half. Using a computer generated perspective view as a basis, you will eventually get a product that looks like it was made by hand.

You can try this technique. You are sure to like it and you will find it of great help when you are pressed for time and up against a deadline, or when you had to hand it in "yesterday". However, keep in mind that this hybrid technique is not pure sketching, and to some degree you are deceiving yourselves. It is justly said that 3D MAX was invented by the people who cannot draw. I am explaining this technique to you so that it might help you to smoothly transition from computer to freehand graphics, to quickly create an interior sketching portfolio, and to have your clients' psyche prepared for it (for not all clients are prepared to appreciate freehand sketching after they have got used to the glossy 3D pictures). By the way, the mentioned above Michelle Morelan has no scruples about admitting in her interviews that she does hybrids and relies on a PC all the time. This, nonetheless, doesn't prevent her from being one of the most successful masters of interior sketching.

As you can understand, I am not opposed to 3D and other computer techniques. Moreover, I myself sometimes use it in my work. It's just that I have come to the conclusion lately that my heart is with hand made drawing. I love drawing and sketching, and I want to share my knowledge of these skills with you. It is a great thing when you are very good at both 3D and freehand technique. This makes you an absolute professional in the eyes of the client and colleagues.

My copy of M. Morelan's work

# 7.3. Advice

At initial stages, when you are just beginning to learn sketching, it is good to have some kind of a step-by-step system, kind of recipe that will speed up your progress.

**After you have mastered the basics, you will get to the juiciest part of it! You will see that anything goes in sketching and you can never go wrong!**

Sketching by definition is about virtuosity and vivacity of performance, suggestive even of audacity and brazenness. Expressiveness is the key quality in sketching. Even if there is something out of the ordinary and is not in accordance with traditional rules, but it's done with confidence, it will be accepted and appreciated. The public will take it as your creative flair, your signature style, your way.

## Universal advice

Try new things, constantly develop, invest in yourself and in your knowledge and skills: study, read books dedicated to sketching and presentation techniques since design, as well as technologies are very rapidly evolving and it is crucial to stay informed. Open-mindedness will insure you against artistic crisis and stagnation. Be open to new knowledge!

# CONCLUSION

This chapter offers you some words of advice and encouragement for the road ahead, reminds you of the great importance of everyday practice and gives you the information about my courses

# Summing-up and farewell words

Dear reader, I hope that you have found the information given in this book useful and inspiring. I am sure that this knowledge will help you to develop you skills and discover your capacity for drawing. If you can ride a bicycle, drive a car, or have learned a foreign language, or found your way around with 3D Max, than you are sure to master sketching, as this is just a skill like the ones above.

You have already learned a lot from this book: how to make a sketch-plan and how to work with it, now you know different kinds of perspectives and have constructed your first frontal perspective – one of the most important for designers, you have become familiar with the basic techniques of masters of sketching as well as hybrid techniques, and you even know what materials you will need to practice sketching.

You will benefit from this book to a far greater degree when you start using the knowledge you have received. So if you read it at first out of curiosity, then, for the second time, use it as a guide and read it with a pencil in hand! It is widely known that we are able to retain in our memory only 10% of the information from reading it for the first time. But if we read and practically use the information, then it is 100% memorized. So, take my advice, read the book once again in the coming weekend. Indeed, the secrets of sketching are right in front of you. The key is to start using them.

Freehand drawing will breathe life and inspiration into your projects. Your customers will see you as a talented artist and will appreciate this special and custom-tailored approach, a 'personal touch'. After the work has been done, they will probably mount your sketches or even will hang them on the wall to adorn their new home. Grateful clients are sure to tell all their friends and acquaintances how happy they were to have such a marvelous and talented designer working on their project.

By the way, when you have collected a sufficient number of sketches, it is good to compile a portfolio of interior design sketches or include them into already existing one. There you can also update your Internet site and social network accounts with the new information, since creating sketches is an additional option, a service which you can now offer to your clients. Most likely in one of my following books I will explain how to create a professional portfolio and the right way to present it to your customer and how go about presenting it to the best possible effect.

Write to me on my site at www.olgaart888.com about which aspects of sketching are of most interest to you, and I will record a master class based on your questions or will cover them in a new book.

# Words of encouragement for the road

Draw every day! Find at least 30 minutes and focus solely on drawing this. This will help you develop your hand, train your ability to judge by eye and develop your sense of proportion and scale. You will be surprised by the result and progress you will achieve thanks to everyday practice. Eventually confidence will emerge in your sketches – the main thing that distinguishes a professional from a beginner. Look at the sketches of the masters – how much strength, livelihood, energy there is in their works. It will all certainly come to you – just practice every day!

If you would like to know more about art of sketching, I recommend watching my lessons and open courses on my YouTube channel "Olga Sorokina". On Instagram account @olgaart888, new information is published every day. I would also be most grateful if you shared your views about this book on your social media, or by sending your comments to me directly.

I wish you creative success! Until next time! I will be looking forward to finding you among the students of my classes.

*Olga Sorokina*

# Appendix: «My 10 Rules of Sketching»

### 1. Foundations of everything

Without a solid knowledge of perspective principles nothing will ever work out. Study the method, refer to the book often and make sure you understand it completely. For the moment concentrate on the frontal perspective - it is very powerful and hugely useful technique.

### 2. Horizon line

Remember, that the horizon line level has effect on the general impression of your sketch. Whether the horizon is at the eye level of a seated person or at 2 meter level above the floor, it is absolutely critical decision for the whole of the drawing and for how different planes are revealed.

### 3. Composition

A well-chosen view angle and the knowledge of composition are most crucial! They will contribute greatly to your sketch; by making your project look elegant and allowing you to present it to the best effect.

### 4. 3D Effect

To be sure, knowledge and application of the rules of light and shadows, the aerial perspective, tonal gradations and texturing are key. It is these things that give volume and expressiveness to a drawing.

## 5. The Trained Eye

Examine as many works and drawings as possible, learn wherever you can: YouTube tutorials or Skillshare classes, drawing exhibitions, read books about design, drawing and illustration. You have to become satiated with visual references for your own new and unique style to take emerge.

## 6. Materials

Use quality materials. You don't need a great number, but let them be the top quality. For a successful start, you will need 7-10 colours of professional markers (with 3-4 of them being tones of grey), a pencil, a black liner, a white pen, an eraser, and paper. Later on, when you start being more involved with sketching, don't pinch the pennies and buy Copic sets.

## 7. Techniques

The classic techniques of sketching will always be in high esteem: this are watercolours, Chinese ink, coloured pencils and pastel. But the experience tells me that the easiest, quickest and the most effective tool in interior sketching is markers: they give wonderful results, even when you use them for the first time.

## 8. Masters

If you want to become proficient at sketching as fast as possible, learn from the masters of the craft: take note of their devices, copy their techniques, and use this rich foundation of knowledge to develop your own unique and inimitable.

## 9. Customers

Remember, that all customers are guided by their emotions when they make decisions, which is why your portfolio and sketches must be "savoury to the eye". Assess your portfolio one more time and ask yourself: «Would I buy it?» If the answer is «No», burn it and make a spectacular instead!

## 10. Everyday practice

Draw every day and train as much as possible your eye and hand. If you start practicing every day for approximately 30 minutes, it will take you about 3 weeks to achieve pretty high mastery of hand and your pictures will start showing confidence - the main quality of a professional, since you can always tell a pro from a beginner by the confidence of their lines and hatchings. Confidence only comes with experience!

Olga Sorokina

# *The* SKETCH

## Interior Design Drawing